Notre-Dame de Paris: The History and Legacy of France's Most Famous Cathedral

By Charles River Editors

An 1830 depiction of Notre-Dame

About Charles River Editors

Charles River Editors is a boutique digital publishing company, specializing in bringing history back to life with educational and engaging books on a wide range of topics. Keep up to date with our new and free offerings with this 5 second sign up on our weekly mailing list, and visit Our Kindle Author Page to see other recently published Kindle titles.

We make these books for you and always want to know our readers' opinions, so we encourage you to leave reviews and look forward to publishing new and exciting titles each week.

Introduction

Maximilien Luce's 1901 painting of Notre-Dame

Notre-Dame

"That most glorious church of the most glorious Virgin Mary, mother of God, deservedly shines out, like the sun among stars. And although some speakers, by their own free judgment, because [they are] able to see only a few things easily, may say that some other is more beautiful, I believe however, respectfully, that, if they attend more diligently to the whole and the parts, they will quickly retract this opinion. Where indeed, I ask, would they find two towers of such magnificence and perfection, so high, so large, so strong, clothed round about with such a multiple variety of ornaments? Where, I ask, would they find such a multipartite arrangement of so many lateral vaults, above and below? Where, I ask, would they find such light-filled amenities as the many surrounding chapels? Furthermore, let them tell me in what church I may see such a large cross, of which one arm separates the choir from the nave. Finally, I would willingly learn where [there are] two such circles, situated opposite each other in a straight line, which on account of their appearance are given the name of the fourth vowel [O] ; among which smaller orbs and circlets, with wondrous artifice, so that some arranged circularly, others angularly, surround windows ruddy with precious colors and beautiful with the most subtle figures of the pictures. In fact I believe that this church offers the carefully discerning such cause for admiration that its inspection can scarcely sate the soul." - Jean de Jandun, *Tractatus de laudibus Parisius*

"Notre Dame de Paris, in particular, is a curious specimen of this variety. Every surface, every stone of this venerable pile, is a page of the history not only of the country, but of science and of art. Thus—to mention here only a few of the chief details—whereas the small Porte Rouge almost touches the limits of fifteenth century Gothic delicacy, the pillars of the nave, by their massiveness and great girth, reach back to the Carlovingian Abbey of Saint-Germain-des-Prés. One would imagine that six centuries lay between that door and those pillars." With these words, the famous 19th century novelist Victor Hugo attempted to introduce his readers to the backdrop of his seminal work, later known as *The Hunchback of Notre Dame*. This, it should be noted, was not the name that Hugo gave to his work; instead, he called it simply *Notre Dame*, after the building in which he set it.

This location was no accident, for, perhaps more than any other city in Europe, Paris has seen every kind of trouble and happiness that can befall a place. It may be called the "City of Lights," but it also frequently saw its leaders' blood spilled in the streets. It is the symbol of romance, but also a place where the famed Napoleon divorced the love of his life in order to have a son. It is famed for its art and culture, but it hosted Nazis during four long years of occupation. Most of all, it is a city of building up and tearing down and building up again, where life is ever-changing.

Yet, in the midst of this history of turmoil and chaos, one place has survived largely unchanged, a symbol to Christian believers of the unchanging truths of faith. Notre-Dame has stood as a monumental, though silent, witness to much of Paris' history. As Hugo pointed out, "This generative Mother-Church is, among the other ancient churches of Paris, a sort of Chimera: she has the head of one, the limbs of another, the body of a third—something of all. These hybrid edifices are, we repeat, by no means the least interesting to the artist, the antiquary, and the historian...They let us realize to how great a degree architecture is a primitive matter, in that they demonstrate...that the greatest productions of architecture are not so much the work of individuals as of a community; are rather the offspring of a nation's labour than the out-come of individual genius; the deposit of a whole people; the heaped-up treasure of centuries; the residuum left by the successive evaporations of human society; in a word, a species of formations. Each wave of time leaves its coating of alluvium, each race deposits its layer on the monuments, each individual contributes his stone to it."

Notre-Dame de Paris: The History and Legacy of France's Most Famous Cathedral chronicles the remarkable history of the Parisian cathedral. Along with pictures depicting important people, places, and events, you will learn about Notre-Dame like never before.

The Origins of the Cathedral

Ancient cities grew up around rivers, those wide, meandering sources of life-giving water and easy transportation, and for Paris, that river is the Seine. It was on the Seine's banks that the conquering Romans raised an altar, not to Christ or his Mother, but to their own god, Jupiter, which they fervently hoped would defend their new city of Lutetia Parisiorum. One 19th century author observed, "The origin of Notre Dame is enveloped in mystery. Whether its first bishop, St. Denisy or Dionysius, was the Areopagite converted by St. Paul's preaching at Athens...or whether he was another personage of the same name who was sent into Gaul in the third century...it is impossible to say.... Certain it is, however, that the first bishop of Paris bore the name of Denis, and that he suffered martyrdom, with his two companions Rusticus and Eleutherius, on the summit of the hill now called Montmartre...An ancient church covered the remains of the three saints until the present splendid building was erected, in the reign of Dagobert I. Under the Roman dominion, Paris was comprised in the fourth Lyonnaise division, of which Sens was the metropolis. Hence the bishops of Paris acknowledged the Archbishop of Sens as their primate until 1622, when, at the request of Louis XIV, Pope Gregory XV raised Paris to the see of an archbishopric."

Writing in 19th century, Augustus Hare observed that in 375, "a church dedicated to St. Stephen, was built under Prudentius, eighth bishop of Paris. In 528, through the gratitude of Childebert...for his recovery from sickness by St. Germain, another far more rich and beautiful edifice arose by the side of the first church, and was destined to become...the cathedral of Paris." He continued, "The new church had not long been finished when La Cite', in which the monks of St. Germain had taken refuge with their treasures, was besieged by the Normans, but it was successfully defended by Bishop Gozlin, who died during the siege. It is believed that the subtractions of this church were found during recent excavations in the Paris Notre Dame...The first stone of a new and much larger cathedral was laid by Pope Alexander III in 1163, under Bishop Maurice de Sully.... The work advanced rapidly. The choir was finished in 1185, and two years later Geoffrey Plantagenet, son of Henry II of England, was buried in front of the high altar."

As is the case with so many churches, the motivation behind Notre-Dame's construction was not entirely pure, as Professor Stephen Murray of Columbia University points out: "The great construction project marks the response of the Metropolitan clergy to at least three kinds of challenge. First, the increasing power of the king of France—translating in turf wars over control of urban topography. Second, the vigorous propagation on the part of the monks of Saint-Denis of the cult of the saint who had become synonymous with Parisian identity. And third, the architectural challenge inherent in the other great churches recently built or under construction: in Normandy and Flanders; and closer at hand, at Senlis where the galleried elevation refers so specifically to Norman sources."

It also seems that the sin of pride may have entered into the equation. Author Sharon Penman noted, "Archeological excavations in the 20th century suggest that this Mérovingian house of worship was massive, with a five-aisled nave similar to that of the first Saint Peter's in Rome. It was some 36 metres wide and at least 70 metres long, and the original foundations lie beneath the present-day cathedral. In 1163, Bishop of Paris Maurice de Sully demolished this Mérovingian basilica to Notre Dame, which had been much altered in the ensuing 650 years. He apparently felt it was not grand enough and wouldn't do to serve as 'the parish church of the kings of Europe…Perhaps he felt the old-fashioned church needed to be updated in the new Gothic style. I think he was also embarrassed that the cathedral of the city of Paris was inferior to Abbot Suger's magnificent Abbaye de St-Denis to the north of the city. Fortunately for us, Sully's competitive feelings eventually resulted in a masterpiece. He devoted his career and fortune to the construction of this cathedral…The land around here had once been filled with other churches, chapels, businesses and residences, but was cleared when Sully began his building campaign. … On the ground are the outlines of some of the old churches and streets that were demolished. There is also a brass star set into the ground right in front of the cathedral that was the "point zero" used to measure the distances of all roads leading to and from Paris."

Cathedrals take decades to build, and this was especially true during the Middle Ages. As a result, they were often completed in stages so that already finished areas could begin to be used. For example, the choir at Notre-Dame, begun in 1163, was completed in 1177, and five years later, the High Altar was consecrated, allowing masses to be held in the church. Both these features were located at the east end of the church.

The east side of the cathedral and its spire

Kurt Muehmel's picture of the choir area

Writing for the *American Spectator* in 2013, Joseph Harris explained, "Like most French cathedrals, Notre Dame de Paris was a long time building. After Pope Alexander III laid the first stone in the presence of King Louis VII in 1163, it took nearly 10 generations of architects, artisans, and laborers to finish the job 182 years later. … Along the way, they had to innovate when the ever higher and thinner load-bearing walls dictated by the new Gothic style, together with larger openings for stained-glass windows, began to fissure. Their solution: the flying buttress. Those dramatic, graceful exterior braces were one of the signatures of the High Gothic style…Conceived on a grand scale to accommodate at least 6,000 worshippers, Notre Dame had a nave 427 feet long and 160 feet wide. Once all the light-gray cut stone was in place, finishing touches were added: vivid colors, now worn away, painted on the façade; grotesque gargoyles set on outside ledges; a 7,800-pipe organ installed in the choir; three stunning, 30-foot rose windows placed in the western façade and north and south transepts; and 20 massive, finely tuned bells hung in two towers."

No man alive at the time could have ever thought that he would live to see such an edifice completed, and when Bishop Sully died in 1196, he was replaced both by Bishop Eudes de Sully (no relation). This Sully was a devotee of form and ritual in the mass and distrusted any pursuit that he considered frivolous. Not only did he continue work on the cathedral, but he also tightened up regulations on the types of extra-religious activities that could take place there.

Architecturally speaking, he supervised the men completing the transepts and the nave. In keeping with the popular trends of that time, painters worked long hours to create a colorful exterior. However, as time passed and the original paint wore away, tastes also changed, and the paint was never restored, leaving the building with the unvarnished stonework seen today. English architectural historian Charles Hiatt noted in 1902, "Notre Dame was the first of the greater French cathedrals in which Gothic principles of construction were logically carried out. The choir was begun in the year the nave (with the exception of the extreme west end) was completed about the year 1195. The west facade was built in the early part of the thirteenth century. Notre Dame is thus older than the cathedral of Amiens, with which one naturally compares it. ... Perhaps we do not overstate the case when we say that the science (as well as the art) of Gothic found its first real expression on a large scale in the Cathedral of Paris."

Jean-Pierre Dalbera's picture of the crypt

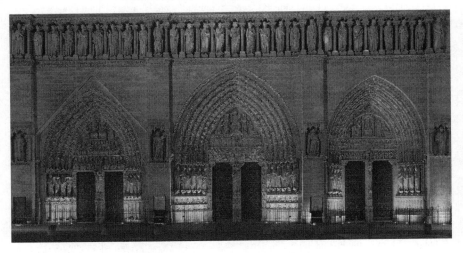

Benh Lieu Song's picture of the façade

Notre Dame's transepts have intrigued more than one architect, and in 1880, Professor Roger Smith wrote of these that "they do not project beyond the line of the side walls, so that, although fairly well-marked in the exterior and interior of the building, they add nothing to its floor-space." He added, "The eastern end of a French cathedral is terminated in an apse. When this apse is encircled by a ring of chapels, with flying buttresses on several stages rising from among them, the whole arrangement is called a chevet, and very striking and busy is the appearance which it presents."

Similarly, Charles Herbert Moore insisted, "A more beautiful eastern termination than the Gothic apse could hardly be conceived. No part of the Romanesque apse, covered with the primitive semi-dome, and enclosed with its simple wall, presented no constructive difficulties, and produced no imposing effect. But the soaring French chevet with its many celled vault, its arcaded stories, its circling aisles and its radial chapels, taxed the utmost inventive power, and entranced the eye of the beholder."

The second Bishop Sully died in 1208, having lived to see the western façade of the building designed but not completed. Caroline Bruzelius explained, "The most secure date for the façade is provided by the destruction in 1208 of several houses belonging to the Hotel-Dieu located on the southeast corner of the parvis, the site where the south portal was to be constructed. Construction of the façade may indeed have been delayed for a number of year while this was being negotiated; certainly, as already remarked, there is good evidence to tie the north side of the façade to a considerably earlier date, when eastern bays of the nave were still underway. This interruption no doubt led to the change in design that was noted by Sauerlander...The construction of the west façade upper stories concentrated on the south tower chamber before the north; the shafts supporting the wall-rib continue to be cut as detached elements there, and the base and plinth profiles are similar to those of the south tribune to the east. Certain details, such as the portals giving access to the tribunes on the north and south, are handled more simply on the south."

Bruzelius also noted that there appeared to be more than one architect working on the building through the years: "This is also true of the trilobed arcading at the top of the spiral stairs in each tower chamber. There is every possibility that the south tower chamber was built by the same master who erected the upper stories on the south side of the nave. The almost complete absence of detached elements on the north, however, indicates the presence of a new, fourth master builder on the scene. He would be the same master who completed the most western nave piers and the wall that rises above them."

The western façade

Later, in the 1240s, sculptor and master mason Jean de Chelles remodeled the famed transepts, adding a gabled entrance to the north transept and installing the magnificent rose window above it. He was assisted by Pierre de Montreuil, who later succeeded him and finished the south transept in a similar style. As a sculptor, de Chelles saw to it that both areas had plenty of sculptures adorning them, including those representing the lives of Christ and various important saints.

Julie Anne Workman's picture of the north rose window

Interestingly enough, at this time the cathedral contained few, if any, of the many chapels that would later grace its interior, but in 1245 workmen were called in to begin to build these small rooms devoted to prayer and contemplation. These proved to be the only significant additions made until the beginning of the 18th century, when, according to one author, "an era of reckless mutilation began."

Some of the most distinctive features of Notre Dame were, and remain, the architects' use of flying buttresses to make the roof higher and more expansive. This was one of the first times that this feature had been used. There is also the matter of the cathedral's exterior beauty, for it was designed with the idea that every possible surface should be decorative. Thus, statues support its rising columns and gargoyles spit out the water that pours off its roof. In fact, those willing to climb the nearly 400 steps the architects put in place for that purpose could reach windows that allow them to see these strange creatures up close and enjoy some of the best views of the city available.

The Middle Ages

The initial iteration of Notre-Dame, built by a Roman, was likely in the Roman style, as excavations through the years have revealed materials likely to have been brought from Rome. Beyond this, however, little about the earliest history of the cathedral can be confirmed.

However, at sometime in the early 13th century a fire swept through the then completed cathedral, doing significant damage. According to one legend, "In 1218 a happy accident gave us the incomparable unity which the Cathedral alone possesses among mediaeval monuments; for in that year, on the eve of the Assumption, four inspired thieves climbed into the roof-tree and warily let down ropes with slip-knots to lasso the silver candlesticks on the altar. These they snared, but as they pulled them up the lights set fire to the hangings that were stretched for the feasts, and the fire spread to the whole choir…"

This is only a legend, for nothing was written about this event, or at least nothing that survived, and it remained for Eugene Viollet-le-Duc to discover the char marks on the walls during his mid-19th century restoration efforts. He believed that, because the church was then such an important part of the community, the repairs were rushed and many former features, such as the rose windows and flying buttresses, were not replaced. The fire did most of its damage to the east side of the building, leaving the west section largely unscathed.

During the next 300 years of "peace," the cathedral experienced its fair share of ups and downs. For instance, St. Dominic himself preached there at least once during the time in which he was establishing his now famous order. According to legend, the Virgin Mary herself appeared to him just before he spoke and gave him the text of his sermon. Toward the end of the 13th century, controversy broke out between the French King (and later saint) Louis IX and the bishop, but the former laid in state in the cathedral in 1271, setting a precedent for future monarchs.

A depiction of Louis IX

Not surprisingly, when the cathedral was finally completed, many happily expressed their opinions on its design. John of Jandun insisted that it was one of the three most important buildings in Paris in 1323: "That most glorious church of the most glorious Virgin Mary, mother of God, deservedly shines out, like the sun among stars. And although some speakers, by their own free judgment, because [they are] able to see only a few things easily, may say that some other is more beautiful, I believe however, respectfully, that, if they attend more diligently to the whole and the parts, they will quickly retract this opinion...Where indeed, I ask, would they find two towers of such magnificence and perfection, so high, so large, so strong, clothed round about with such a multiple variety of ornaments? Where, I ask, would they find such a multipartite arrangement of so many lateral vaults, above and below? Where, I ask, would they find such light-filled amenities as the many surrounding chapels? Furthermore, let them tell me in what church I may see such a large cross, of which one arm separates the choir from the nave…Finally, I would willingly learn where [there are] two such circles, situated opposite each other in a straight line, which on account of their appearance are given the name of the fourth vowel; among which smaller orbs and circlets, with wondrous artifice, so that some arranged circularly, others angularly, surround windows ruddy with precious colors and beautiful with the most subtle figures of the pictures. In fact I believe that this church offers the carefully discerning such cause for admiration that its inspection can scarcely sate the soul."

Over the next 100 years, the rest of the cathedral was completed, assuring its central place in the life of the people of Paris, but things were turbulent in France itself. King Charles VI nearly found himself lying in state before his time, for, on January 28, 1393, he nearly burned to death after a fire broke out at what was known as the "Ball of the Wild Men." Four of his courtiers were killed and the young king's authority was gravely undermined by the incident, forcing him to make a great show of penance and gratitude at the cathedral for what many believed was his miraculous survival.

The French court continued to suffered hardships until the nation finally suffered defeat at the hands of the English King Henry V at Agincourt in 1415. Five years later, in 1420, Henry V briefly solidified his right to the throne by marrying Charles's daughter, Catherine. Following their nuptials, he visited the cathedral, where, a mere two years later, his infant son, Henry VI, was crowned king of France. As fate would have it, the child's reign proved short-lived and the English were soon driven out, leading to yet another great celebration at Notre-Dame when Charles VII rose to power.

King Charles VI

King Charles VII

Even the peaceful years were not without their important events, and one of the strangest of which occurred in 1450. As the city grew, many of the wild animals living in the surrounding forests were left homeless or forced to live closer together than they had previously had to. This was particularly hard on the wolf population, especially because the residents of Paris were also hunting in the forests and killing much of the game that the wolves commonly depended on for food. Driven by hunger and fear, these natural predators began to make incursions into the city, killing livestock and sometimes, so the rumors went, attacking human beings. As the rumors spread, so did the terror, until finally the people of Paris united to fight back. They closed in the square in front of Notre-Dame with barricades and went out hunting the wolves, not attempting to kill them but instead to drive the pack into the square. Once the entire pack was trapped, a large crowd of people ran out and surrounded them, spearing and clubbing them to death. Thrilled with what they had done, the citizens then carried the dead body of the lead wolf, whom they called Courtaud, around the city in triumph.

If this seems unnecessarily cruel, the Middle Ages were cruel times, especially when judged by modern standards. For instance, less that 20 years earlier, the French people burned a 19 year old girl named Joan at the stake, even after she had saved the country in battle. It was only small comfort to her family that the people soon regretted their decision and even awarded a pension to Joan of Arc's mother, Isabelle Romee, in honor of her daughter's service to the nation. Romee wanted more and on November 7, 1455, she appeared at Notre-Dame to testify on her daughter's behalf at Joan's Trial of Nullification or Rehabilitation. She stated, "I had a daughter born in lawful wedlock who grew up amid the fields and pastures. I had her baptized and confirmed and brought her up in the fear of God. I taught her respect for the traditions of the Church as much as I was able to do given her age and simplicity of her condition. I succeeded so well that she spent much of her time in church and after having gone to confession she received the sacrament of the Eucharist every month…Because the people suffered so much, she had a great compassion for them in her heart and despite her youth she would fast and pray for them with great devotion and fervor. She never thought, spoke or did anything against the faith…Certain enemies had her arraigned in a religious trial. Despite her disclaimers and appeals, both tacit and expressed, and without any help given to her defense, she was put through a perfidious, violent, iniquitous and sinful trial. The judges condemned her falsely, damnably and criminally, and put her to death in a cruel manner by fire. For the damnation of their souls and in notorious, infamous and irreparable loss to me, Isabelle, and mine..."

The Joan of Arc statue in Notre-Dame

The court heard Romee's words and those of the other witnesses and overturned Joan's conviction in 1456. It went further, declaring her in fact to be a martyr of the Catholic faith and opening the door for her future canonization.

At this time, French kings were generally crowned at Rheims, but they soon made their way to formal Thanksgiving services at Notre-Dame. Also, England and France made yet another attempt at permanent peace in 1514, when Louis XII married Henry VIII's sister, Mary, in the cathedral. According to 19th century author W. N. Lonergan, "In the annals of Notre Dame from the days of Louis XI , the rebellious dauphin who succeeded his father, Charles VII, to the reign of the fourteenth Louis, there is chiefly a long record of Te Deums after the victories of the

French army. Historic Rheims, where Clovis had been baptized by S. Remi in 496, was the favored city of the Merovingians, who had accorded it great privileges."

Entering the Modern Era

In order to fully appreciate the role of Notre-Dame during the time of the Protestant Reformation, one must understand the role of the church and state in 16th century Europe, that is, they were nearly one and the same, at least to the extent that no monarch could hope to remain in power for any length of time without the approval or at least passive support of the churches in the nation. Because it was not just a symbol of French power, but also of the rule of the Catholic Church in France, Notre-Dame soon became a target for violence during the Reformation, and the peace of the church was again interrupted when, in 1548, a mob of French Huguenots, members of newly coined Protestantism, attacked the cathedral. The mob, inflamed by the words of John Calvin against the Catholic Church, destroyed statues that they claimed the Catholic parishioners worshiped, and wreaked havoc wherever they could. Fortunately, they were soon stopped and much of the damage they did was restored.

Of course, Notre-Dame was much more than a symbol of God's authority; it also symbolized His presumed approval of the actions of those reigning over the nation, thus shoring up the important principle of the "divine right of kings." To this end, monarchs used the cathedral as the backdrop for their most important personal events, in particular weddings and baptisms. Marriages were contracted with the leaders of other nations in order to guarantee peace, at least for a while, and the baptisms of heirs to the throne, as well as their younger siblings, opened the door to increased power.

One of the most important marriages to ever take place in Notre-Dame occurred between two teenagers in 1558. 15 year old Mary was already the Queen of Scotland and had been since she was a week old, while Francis, at 17, was the dauphin of France but would one day reign for a few short years as Francis II. According to Mary's biographer, Thomas Finlayson Henderson, "The marriage itself followed on Sunday, April 24th, in the Cathedral of Notre Dame, gorgeously decorated for the occasion a Vantique. The Bishop of Paris received the young couple at the porch under a royal canopy of fleur de lis and addressed to them a discourse; but the nuptial ceremony was performed by the Cardinal Charles de Bourbon, who, we are told, pronounced the sacramental words that united them in marriage, with a reverence and dignity 'qu'il est impossible de le dire.'...For the French court and for Paris the occasion was of quite exceptional interest, because no Dauphin had been married at home for more than two hundred years. Then the marriage was in reality the celebration of a great triumph of French diplomacy, and seemed to inaugurate a new era of French glory."

Francis and Mary

With the spread of the Protestant faith in Europe, the matter of marriages among monarchs became trickier, as France soon wanted to form alliances with nations whose leaders were no longer Catholic. At the same time, it was important to most of the people of the nation that their own royal family continue in what they felt was the one true faith. To this end, those in power had to strike a careful balance when it came time for their children to wed. For instance, when Henry of Navarre came to Paris in 1572 to marry Margaret of Valois, Francis II's sister, he could not be married in the cathedral proper because he was not Catholic, so instead he and Margaret married in the parvis, the front courtyard of Notre-Dame. The following year, he returned to the cathedral to vow publicly that he would respect the rights of all Christians to practice their faith.

While the cathedral did often suffer at the hands of those wishing it harm, damage was also perpetrated by those trying to improve its architecture. For instance, in the early 17th century, the famous "Sun King," Louis XIV, launched a campaign of renovation that did its own fair share of damage. To be clear, his intentions were the best, and he wrote on February 10, 1638 a

"Declaration of the King by which His Majesty declares that he has adopted the very holy and glorious Virgin as the special protectress of his kingdom." Part of it read, "We have declared and declare that, taking the most holy and glorious Virgin as the special protectress of our kingdom, we consecrate to her in a particular way our person, our State, our crown and our subjects, beseeching her to inspire us to behave in a holy manner and to so diligently defend this kingdom against the endeavours of all its enemies that, whether it suffers the plague of war or enjoys the sweetness of peace, we implore God from the depth of our heart, that it may never depart from the path of grace leading to the path of glory."

Jean-Pierre Cartier, emeritus professor at Lycée Hoche of Versailles, observed in 2016, "In promulgating the vow as the fundamental law of the kingdom recorded by the Parliament of Paris, Louis XIII undertook to ensure its continuance throughout the centuries, notably by the installation of a new high altar dedicated to the Virgin in Notre Dame Cathedral, in which she would be depicted holding in her arms the body of her Son descended from the Cross, thus marking the profound connection between the Incarnation and the Redemption. In 1698, Louis XIV requested Mgr Louis-Antoine de Noailles…to study a new embellishment for the cathedral, under the supervision of Jules Hardouin-Mansart, First Architect to the King, in order to fulfil his father's vow."

The Archbishop of Paris laid the first stone for the new altar on December 7, 1699. Unfortunately, as Cartier explained, "due to the considerable expenditure incurred in connection with the War of the Spanish Succession…, Louis XIV no longer had the financial resources for the works necessary to fulfil the vow. And so, in 1703, the work initially planned was simplified and it was decided to create a high altar located at the bottom of the choir, and in particular to abandon the baldachin initially planned. In 1708, the exceptional donation by Canon Antoine de le Porte…allowed works to be resumed under the direction of Robert de Cotte, who had become First Architect to the King. The work would last until 1725…The actual vow was fulfilled by the creation of a very beautiful Baroque group of three statues of excellent quality. In the centre a Virgin of Pity, the work of Nicolas Coustou, depicted Mary at the foot of the Cross in tears before the body of Jesus…. On the right, the statue of King Louis XIII can be seen kneeling and handing his crown and sceptre to Mary. … On the other side of the Pietà, a magnificent work by Antoine Coysevox depicts King Louis XIV as a 'very Christian' king with his hand on his heart, assuring Mary of his faithfulness."

In 1699, the king ordered an addition to the church, and the cornerstone laid by the Archbishop read, "Louis the Great — son of Louis the Just — after he had suppressed heresy, established the true faith in his kingdom, terminated gloriously wars by land and sea, wishing to accomplish the vow of his father, built this altar in the cathedral church of Paris, dedicating it to the God of Arms, Master of Peace and Victory, under the invocation of the Virgin, patron and protector of his State."

In the late 1720s, Boffrand, architect for the king, repaired the ceiling and the rose window in the south transept. However, this work did not remain in place, and one author later complained, "The pair of arches leading to the choir aisles with their elaborate crocheted canopies are somewhat feebly contrived in both transepts. The clustered shafts are clumsily arranged. The details on the north side differ from those on the south. On the east and west sides of both transepts there are two narrow bays of the triforium. The clerestory consists of short pointed windows with wheel windows beneath them. This is due to Viollet-le-Duc, and is intended to show us the arrangement which obtained throughout the church previous to the alterations which resulted from the fire in the thirteenth century."

During the 18th century, an architect named Soufflot created what many Notre-Dame historians believed to be some sort of architectural blasphemy by removing the lower portion of the tympanum so that the massive processions that were popular during that period could move through more easily. The tympanum in question was originally devoted to the Last Judgment, which, according to one author, showed "the elect joyfully glancing heavenwards, while on the left the grinning demons haul a row of chained souls to hell. Crowning all is seen the Redeemer, showing the wounds in His hands. Near Him are two angels, and behind the Virgin and St. John the Evangelist interceding on their knees for fallen humanity. As a setting to this magnificent composition are six rows of sculptured forms, making a voussure or set of curves, with figures of prophets, doctors, martyrs, devils, toads, damned souls, and a hideous ape with crooked toes and fingernails. Some of the ornamentation of the six ranges of arch curves is gruesome and _ terrible. It relates either to the celestial or infernal results of the last judgment."

Like most churches in France, Notre Dame suffered much at the hands of the leaders of the French Revolution. Citizen Chaumette and Citizen Dupuis used their influence to protect the massive structure, but while the building itself survived, it was in many ways a hollow victory, since the principles and faith for which it stood took a terrible beating. For instance, on November 10, 1793, priests who wanted to live had to renounce their Catholic faith and instead embrace the principle of "no Religion but Liberty." On that day, according to Carlyle, "Most of these people were still drunk, with the brandy they had swallowed out of chalices; – eating mackerel on the patenas! Mounted on Asses, which were housed with Priests' cloaks, they reined them with Priests' stoles; they held clutched with the same hand communion-cup and sacred wafer. They stopped at the doors of Dram-shops; held out ciboriums: and the landlord, stoop in hand, had to fill them thrice. Next came Mules high-laden with crosses, chandeliers, censers, holy-water vessels, hyssops; – recalling to mind the Priests of Cybele, whose panniers, filled with the instruments of their worship, served at once as storehouse, sacristy, and temple. In such equipage did these profaners advance towards the Convention. They enter there, in an immense train, ranged in two rows; all masked like mummers in fantastic sacerdotal vestments; bearing on hand-barrows their heaped plunder, – ciboriums, suns, candelabras, plates of gold and sliver."

During these "festivities," Notre Dame was declared the temple of the nation's new religion, the "Cult of Reason." Carlyle later added, "Nay, were it too much of an august National Representation that it also went with us to the ci-devant Cathedral called of Notre Dame, and executed a few strophes in worship of her ? ... And now after due pause and flourishes of oratory, the Convention, gathering its limbs, does get under way in the required procession towards Notre Dame...Reason, again in her litter, sitting in the van of them, borne, as one judges, by men in the Roman costume ; escorted by wind-music, red nightcaps, and the madness of the world. And so, straightway. Reason taking seat on the high-altar of Notre Dame, the requisite worship or quasi-worship is, say the Newspapers, executed, National Convention chanting 'the Hymn to Liberty,' words by Chenier, music by Gossee. It is the first of the Feasts of Reason, first communion-service of the New Religion of Chaumette."

Apparently the members of the Cult of Reason had no interest in "higher reasoning," for they soon removed the spire that had been placed at the top of the cathedral in its early days to draw men's eyes and hearts toward heaven. Tiring perhaps of beheading humans, they also took their tools to the statues of the Kings and Judah that adorned the cathedral's ledge, cutting off their heads and throwing them in a trash heap, where they lay for nearly 200 years before being discovered during an archeological excavation.

Perhaps the most symbolic blasphemy occurred when France's new leaders replaced the statue of the Virgin Mary, the traditional guardian of the city, with one of Lady Liberty, the country's new guardian. In 1794, those in power turned Paris' magnificent cathedral into a storage house for food and an 18th century liquor store, using Notre-Dame as a venue to sell off wine they had taken from those they killed or forced to flee the country. Then, in May, it became the "Temple of the Supreme Being," after Robespierre led the government to agree that there was a "consoling principle of the Immortality of the Soul." This did not last long, however, and as soon as Robespierre fell from power in 1795, the building was again turned over to the Catholic Church for use in worship.

The 19th Century

While he may have not been particularly religious himself, Napoleon Bonaparte, like his predecessors, recognized the value of religious activity in the lives of his subjects, and so Notre-Dame remained undisturbed during his time in power. Since the French emperor also recognized the value of a magnificent backdrop for his ceremonies, he chose it as the location for his all-important coronation in 1804. However, it seems that perhaps the building itself had something to say about the new emperor's impertinence in seizing the crown from the pope and placing it on his head himself, for the Duchess of Abrantes later wrote, "For several months previous to the coronation, the ancient roof and walls of Notre- Dame had been unmercifully hammered by the workmen employed in fixing up the decorations: and several small particles of stone which had been thus loosened fell during the ceremony into the nave and choir. Just at the moment when Napoleon seized the crown, and placed it on his-own head, a stone, about the size of a nut, fell from the roof, directly over the Emperor's shoulder. There was no movement or gesture of the

Emperor, which could enable me to guess whether or not he felt the stone touch him; bat small as it was, considering the vast height from which it fell, it is scarcely possible to believe he could be unconscious of the circumstance."

A painting depicting the coronation

After Waterloo ended Napoleon's reign, Louis XVIII celebrated his rise to power, and his family's return to the throne, by attending mass at Notre-Dame. Likewise, when the Napoleonic dynasty came back into power, the family held a mass to celebrate the return of Napoleon I, or more precisely, his remains, to France.

Then, in the mid-1840s, Eugene Viollet-le-Duc and Jean-Baptiste-Antoine Lassus began the most significant restoration efforts to date. They worked on the cathedral for a full quarter century, adding a taller spire and various chimeras to accompany the already famous gargoyles. They also updated the transepts, with Viollet later writing, "At the four angles of the crossing, massive piers, some covered with combined pilasters, others with clustered columns, rise without a break from the ground to the vaulting. The two transepts at the outset were only of two bays similar to those of the nave. They were lengthened by a shallower bay when the facades were rebuilt. The later bays are easily distinguished from the four older ones. Thin round vaulting-ribs cross at a crown deeper and more pronounced than those of the older parts. The north and south doors are set in a rich arcading, of which the divisions and the tympanums can be compared to nothing more fitly than a large window with mullions...In the south transept, statues more or less mutilated, representing Christ and the saints, remain at the points of the gables. In describing the exterior of the facades we pointed out the open gallery which extends the whole breadth of each transept, and the great rose window a little above it. The exterior arcading of the gallery is repeated by a similar arcading inside. There is a passage between the two rows of little columns, and there is another above this. The effect of the rose windows in the interior, with glowing stained glass in all their compartments, recalls the marvelous descriptions that Dante has given us of the circles of Paradise. The incomparable splendor alternately astonishes and enchants us. To decorate the side walls of his bays, Jean de Chelles continued the arcading and the mullioned windows."

Even in its heyday, Notre-Dame's architecture did not enjoy universal popularity. A Victorian era architect named P. G. Hamerton insisted, "The great west front, where the towers are, is one of the chief architectural glories of France. There is hardly any work of architecture in the whole world...which has evoked the same kind and degree of admiration as the west front of Notre Dame. It is considered to be one of those rarest products of consummate genius in which imagination of the highest kind works in perfect accordance with the most severe reason. May I confess frankly that until I had carefully studied it under the guidance of Viollet-le-Duc, the front of Notre Dame never produced upon me the same effect as the west fronts of some other French cathedrals of equal rank? I believe the reason to be that Notre Dame is not so picturesque as some others, and does not so much excite the imagination as they do. It is well ordered, and a perfectly sane piece of work...but it has not the imaginative intricacy of Rouen, nor the rich exuberance of Amiens and Reims, nor the fortress-like grandeur of Bourges, nor the elegant variety of Chartres. A man of very high architectural attainments would probably value the romantic element less than I do, simply because much that seems rich and imaginative to an amateur in architecture is understood too quickly in all its details by a master for it to produce the same poetic feeling in his mind...The truth is that the virtues of the west front of Notre Dame are rather classic than romantic. Everything in it seems the result of perfect knowledge and consummate calculation. There are none of those mistakes which generally occur in works of wilder genius. Storey after storey the massive front rears itself to the towers, every resting-place for the eye or as an attraction."

The 20th Century

Writing at the turn of the 20th century, Charle Hiatt claimed, "The great festivals of the Church are celebrated at Notre Dame on a scale of almost unrivalled magnificence. On Assumption Day, in particular, splendid music, wedded to the most ornate ritual, produces an effect never to be forgotten. The pulpit of the metropolitan cathedral has been occupied by a succession of great preachers, amongst them Bossuet and Bourdaloue, and the services and conferences are noted throughout the Roman Catholic world...The Dominican Lacordaire began in 1835 series of majestic and picturesque discourses, which earned for him the title le Romantique de la Chaire and he has been described as filling as a preacher the place occupied in literature by Victor Hugo and in painting by Delacroix.... In recent times among the most popular pulpit orators have been the fiery Jesuit Pere Ravignan, Monseigneur d'Hulst, Pere Monsabr and...Pere Hyacinthe."

Around that time, something occurred that would forever alter the character of Notre-Dame. In 1905, the government formally took possession of the cathedral, based on its history of supporting the Roman Catholic Church as the State Church of France. Though the state made the Catholic Church a perpetual beneficiary of the building, the French government is responsible for maintaining the building and deciding what, if any, changes could be made to it.

The government would soon find that it desperately needed the spiritual strength the cathedral represented as it was drawn into World War I. On October 12, 1914, the wire services reported, "A score of bombs launched on different quarters of Paris by two German aviators today killed three civilians and injured 14 others. ... The second aero plane also flew over the cathedral, dropping four bombs, one of which lighted on the roof of the church, but failed to explode. A second fell on the square where the bishop's residence is located. A third struck the parapet of the Qualde Bourbon and glanced off in the Seine. The fourth disappeared in the Seine near the bridge of Notre Dame...The second aeroplane appeared to aim at the cathedral. While the other machine attempted to hit the Northern and St. Lasara stations. Altogether 20 bombsfell. The Germans flew at a very low altitude. After they apparently had exhausted their supply of missiles, French airmen ascended and pursued the Germans toward the east. A pennant which was dropped at the same time as the bombs from the German airships bore the inscription In German: 'We have taken Antwerp: your turn will soon come.' Of the Injured, 12 were women and girls."

While people find it easy enough to believe that Notre Dame could be the site of coronations and baptisms, it is much harder to believe that it has, on more than one occasion, been chosen as a site for suicide. The most famous of these occurred on February 11, 1931, when Antonieta Rivas Mercado, known by her Anglicized name in the newspapers, shot herself. The press reported, "The stillness of Notre Dame was shattered by a revolver shot to-day. When the clergy hurried to a confessional, they found Mrs. Antoinette Blair dying, holding in her hand a letter addressed to the Mexican Consul-General, notifying him of her intention to commit suicide. Blair and his wife were wealthy, the former being a Scottish merchant, who is now in Mexico. It is understood that divorce proceedings were pending against Mrs. Blair. The cathedral was closed for three hours for reconsecration."

But there was more to the story, for Mercado was no anonymous individual driven to despair by life's circumstances. Instead, she was the daughter of an important Mexican architect and had been married to a prominent engineer. She was active in cultural and arts circles in Mexico and wrote for a number of magazines. It seems that her failed love affair with politician José Vasconcelos is what finally pushed her over the edge and led her to take her life.

People often go to churches to celebrate and commemorate births and deaths, but either rarely happened happen in the church itself. However, there are exceptional events that seem to be almost the stuff of legend. One of these occurred in June 1937, when the famed organist and conductor Louis Vierne died at his post at the grand organ in Notre Dame. Writing in 2012 for the *Huffington Post*, organist Christopher Houlihan recounted the story: "Vierne was organist at the Cathedral of Notre Dame in Paris, where, after nearly 37 years of working there, the clergy decided that organ recitals were no longer going to be allowed. However, one final recital was scheduled for June 2nd, 1937, supposedly the 1,750th performance of Vierne's career. …Vierne was not in good shape, physically or emotionally. He was smoking three packs of cigarettes a day, taking tranquilizers, sleeping pills, and inhaling ether when he felt nervous. He was depressed, and lonely. But, on June 2nd, a reported 3,000 people gathered to hear the famous organist of Notre Dame perform. Vierne could barely climb the many steps up to the organ loft, and a doctor even gave him heart stimulant pills to help…The program began with one of his own compositions. By the end of the work, Vierne was reportedly clutching at the keys. No one in the cathedral, apart from the very few gathered around Vierne high up in the organ loft, could see what was happening. Next, he was programed to improvise (something French organists are famous for). Vierne adjusted many stops of the organ, choosing the sounds he wanted to hear. "I'm going to be ill," he said to his student Maurice Duruflé, who was standing beside him. Then, the 3,000 in the audience, far below the organ loft, heard a low note come from the organ: the start of the improvisation, they assumed. But right then, Vierne had a heart attack. His foot landed on low E of the pedalboard — the last note he ever played. He died just a few short moments later…It's not an entirely depressing story. The great thing is, Vierne had always said that was exactly where he hoped he would die — at the keyboards of the instrument he loved. The organ bench he was sitting on is even on display in the organ loft at Notre Dame to this day."

Eric Chan's picture of the organ

One of the most famous people in the world came to tour the city of Paris for the first time on June 28, 1940. Over the next three hours, he rode through the city's streets, stopping to tour L'Opéra Paris. He rode down the Champs-Élysées toward the Trocadero and the Eiffel Tower, where he had his picture taken. After passing through the Arc de Triomphe, he toured the Pantheon and old medieval churches, though he did not manage to see the Louvre or the Palace of Justice. Heading back to the airport, he told his staff, "It was the dream of my life to be permitted to see Paris. I cannot say how happy I am to have that dream fulfilled today." Four years after his tour, Adolf Hitler would order the city's garrison commander, General Dietrich von Choltitz, to destroy Paris, warning his subordinate that the city "must not fall into the enemy's hand except lying in complete debris."

Wars are known for generating heroic actions on the part of soldiers on both sides of the conflict, but sometimes heroism takes the form of only not doing as badly as one might otherwise do. Such, it seems, was the case with von Cholitz, who took command of Paris following D-Day. According to his son, Timo, "If he saved only Notre Dame, that would be enough reason for the French to be grateful. But he could have done a lot more. France officially refuses to this day to accept it and insists that the Resistance liberated Paris with 2,000 guns against the German army. To official France, my father was swine, but every educated French person knows what he did for them. I am very proud of his memory. ... My father was a professional soldier. But he was no Nazi. He hated Hitler and, when they met, realised he had gone crazy."

General Dietrich von Cholitz

A 2004 article in *The Telegraph* supports this claim, with the author insisting, "But if the German army was, by late August 1944, incapable of flattening the capital as it had Warsaw, it is clear that Gen von Choltitz could have ordered mass killings and the blowing up of historic buildings. ... Gen von Choltitz took command in Paris on Aug 8, 1944, after witnessing his troops suffer dreadful casualties in Normandy. At a meeting in Germany the day before, Hitler told him to be prepared to leave no religious building or historic monument standing. He confirmed the order by cable, telling Gen von Choltitz to turn the city into a 'pile of rubble'".

Having endured the war, Notre-Dame earned the right to rejoice in the peace. On August 25, 1944, a reporter described Paris' joy upon being liberated: "As I write this there are bursts from machine guns and machine gun pistols outside my hotel on Boulevard St. Michel leading down to Notre Dame cathedral. Notre Dame cathedral itself is not damaged. Paris as a whole appears to have suffered only slightly from war. ... And tonight while bullets still were whining around Paris, Parisians were singing in the street...."

Limited time and resources were devoted to more pressing repairs around Paris in the wake of World War II, but even so, the cathedral continued to serve as the backdrop for numerous public events. In the postwar period, one of the most striking was the Requiem Mass of Charles de Gaulle. "President Nixon and Soviet President Nikolai Podgorny were among the more than 100 presidents, kings and prime ministers at the services in Notre Dame, bathed in sunlight today for the first time since De Gaulle died on Monday night. The bells of the thousand year-old cathedral tolled a knell and the sound was taken up by the 40,000 churches of France— the first national bell ringing since they pealed when France was liberated from the Nazis in World War II. ... With the sound today De Gaulle passed into history as he had instructed in his last testament— tributes in Paris from the statesmen he had both provoked and pleased and an outpouring of emotion from the simple folk seeing him to his grave in the champagne hills of Colombey."

Throughout this time, the people of Paris never forgot about the cathedral, even if many were no longer as fervently Catholic. In times of unrest, as Parisians sought to find a place in the changing world, they would determine what role the old cathedral would play in the new culture. As time passed, the church became less about its traditional Catholic faith and more about a sort of cultural spirituality. It also lost the respect that it had enjoyed in previous years as a house of worship. For instance, in 1971, the Associated Press reported an unusual event with the headline "Notre Dame Scene of Tightrope Walk." The article told readers, "A little man in black danced against the gray Paris sky Saturday, looking down and laughing from a tightrope strung between the two towers of Notre Dame Cathedral. He juggled balls, pranced back and forth and lay down on the cable 225 feet above the ground. A crowd applauded and the police, feeling a bit silly, gave up on bringing the man down after trying to find winches, ropes and rescue specialists. The tightrope walker turned out to be Philippe Petit, 21, a professional. He descended on his own. The police were a little confused about how Petit set up his equipment. An officer said he had helpers because the cable stretched between the two towers weighed more than 100 pounds. Petit was taken to a nearby police precinct for an identity check." And, with a wink and a nod to history, "Traditionally, the cathedral, built from 1163 to 1345, has been a home for jugglers and acrobats who crowded outside its main entrance during the Middle Ages."

At no point in its history has Notre-Dame been immune from the impact of social and political upheaval, but in the years following the confusion brought about by Vatican II and the hippie movement, those in charge of the great cathedral must have thought that they were once more facing something akin to the desperate days of the French Revolution. In September 1975, the *United Press International* reported, "Notre Dame Cathedral and its vast square have become this summer's evening music and marijuana hangout for thousands of young people from all over the world. ... The sweet smell of marijuana drifted over Viviani Square to mingle with the odors of Incense and candles wafting from the cathedral. ... As dawn's light touched the rose window of the 700-year-old Gothic cathedral, the story of the night littered the square: empty wine and beer bottles, cigarette stubs, contraceptives, crumpled paper caps. Pigeons pecked at rotting apple cores and hunks of bread."

The cause was, as is so often the case, an unintended consequence of progress. The article observed, "Viviani Square was cleared of cars and turned into a pedestrian mall last year after an underground parking lot was built - the first time the area in front of Notre Dame had been clear since its construction began in 1263. In less time than it takes to knock off a liter of red wine, the French and foreign youths who mill around the Latin Quarter in the summer discovered that the cathedral square was a nifty place to gather."

Weighing in on the situation, Father Naz, a member of the staff of the cathedral, complained, "The youth certainly are not there to re-enact the passion of Christ as youth did in the Middle Ages. They organized a drug traffic. Last night a dozen Congolese and Gabonese immigrants were selling African rings and bracelets. This morning when I came at 7:30 I counted 29 sleeping bags on the square. The police must be on vacation, too." He also told how, on Ascension Day, while worshippers from around the world were praying, "Suddenly a thousand young people ran into the church from the square with their trombones, guitars and tom-toms. They blocked the door and people could not leave. There was nothing we could do…young people were using the square for illegal camping. I have seen English and Dutch out there making coffee with gas cookers. In French cities 'le picnic' is forbidden. The police have become very gracious, to foreigners, I must say."

In the end, the cathedral showed that it could take care of itself: "But the blue-jeaned youths milling on the square get their come-uppance from Notre Dame each evening when the 13-ton great bell in the south tower bongs its seven-centuries-old call to evening mass."

By the time John Paul II became pope in 1979, the Catholic Church was a ready for a change, and ready to restore some of its sacred traditions. The following year, on May 31, 1980, the new pontiff launched his global appeal for a return to traditional values at Notre-Dame. The *Associated Press* covered the story: "The church bells of Paris pealed a welcome to Pope John Paul II on Friday and hundreds of thousands of people lined the route to Notre Dame Cathedral, where he celebrated Mass at the spiritual heart of France's faith. ... From the huge square he drove along the Boulevard St. Germain, cheered by the crowds on his way to the 816-year-old

Cathedral of Notre Dame de Paris. Entering the cathedral, the pope broke protocol to walk among the aisles. He donned a scarlet vest and sat in a plush chair on the carpeted marble altar to listen to a greeting from bespectacled Cardinal Francois Marty, archbishop of Paris and his old friend…The 100-foot high church beams shook to the thunderous music of Notre Dame's organ, kettle drums and a choir of a thousand voices, and John Paul led a Te Deum — a hymn of thanks to God. Then under a sky grown cloudy but broken occasionally by the sun, he celebrated Mass for a crowd of about 15,000 persons jammed into the small square in front of the cathedral."

War and controversy are one thing, but one the greatest dangers to Notre-Dame proved to be time and weather. In 1991, the *Associated Press* told readers, "Old age, pollution and the elements have caught up with Notre Dame, the noble Gothic cathedral often called 'the parish of French history.' … The ministry has allocated about $ 19 million for an ambitious 10-year facelift scheduled to begin this summer. …rain, wind, sun, frost and dust have eaten away the porous gray stone over the centuries. Restoration will begin with removal of all loose stones and installation of more nets to catch any that fall. Chunks of loose stone regularly fall from the facade and interior walls, some into nets and others near visitors…Notre Dame's most dangerous enemy is pollution from the hundreds of taxis and tourist buses that visit the cathedral each day on the Ile de la Cite in the middle of the Seine. Fonquemic said many buses park for hours with motors running, and exhaust spewing, for the sole purpose of maintaining heat in winter and air conditioning in summer. City authorities banned parking around the cathedral in 1989, but the rule is widely ignored and few vehicles are towed away. Eleven million visitors a year also have taken their toll. Sweaty hands soil the walls and footsteps wear the floors."

Architect Bernard Fonquemic, who would head up the project, insisted, "The monument's general condition is worrisome, and if we don't do something now, we'll end up with a very sick building. … Last year, freezing temperatures caused a lot of damage. In the spring, many fragments broke loose. … I have seen the stained glass windows, vaults and pillars dripping with condensation caused by the heat of human bodies. … For me, this is a real problem. How authentic will Notre Dame be when its stones have been replaced?"

On May 21, 2013, the peace of the cathedral was once again shattered by violence when another visitor chose to end his life in her sacred halls. The *Associated Press* wrote, "Some 1,500 visitors were cleared out of Notre Dame Cathedral in Paris after a man put a letter on the altar of the 850- year-old monument Tuesday, pulled out a gun and shot himself in the head. It's the first suicide in decades at the landmark site, Monsignor Patrick Jacquin, the cathedral's rector, told The Associated Press. 'It's unfortunate, it's dramatic, it's shocking,' Jacquin said…The motives for the suicide, and the contents of the man's letter, were unclear. The Paris prosecutor's office identified the man as 78-year-old Dominique Venner. Venner's blog describes him as a historian and essayist…. It says he fought with French forces against Algerian independence fighters a half-century ago in a war that ended with France losing its most prized colony."

Venner, it turns out, was more than just another person committing suicide. He had been a member of the Secret Army Organiation (OAS), which had waged a campaign against the French withdrawal from Algeria in the early 1960s. After this, he became a prominent right-wing nationalist who railed against what he saw as the decadence of liberal democracy as a member of the European New Right, a loose collection of like-minded writers and philosophers. Eventually he soured on politics and concentrated on his historical studies. He wrote of his reasons for committing suicide at the cathedral in a note he left: "I am healthy in body and mind, and I am filled with love for my wife and children. I love life and expect nothing beyond, if not the perpetuation of my race and my mind. However, in the evening of my life, facing immense dangers to my French and European homeland, I feel the duty to act as long as I still have strength. I believe it necessary to sacrifice myself to break the lethargy that plagues us. I give up what life remains to me in order to protest and to found. I chose a highly symbolic place, the Cathedral of Notre Dame de Paris, which I respect and admire: she was built by the genius of my ancestors on the site of cults still more ancient, recalling our immemorial origins."

A Parisian Hotspot

While most people visit Notre-Dame to admire its architecture, those who stay to hear its magnificent pipe organ played are rarely disappointed. However, it was not always so, for the first organs installed were far from adequate for the building's size and the crowds that it attracted, especially on feat days. It was only in the mid-18th century that Francois-Henri Clicquot built a new organ for the cathedral, installing some of the pipes that are still in use today. However, these would also not go unmolested for long. In 2013, an *Associated Press* article reported on "the weight of history" that the instrument bears: "There are deep gashes in the wood carvings of the organ loft — a legacy of revolutionaries from the late 18th century who slashed away the fleur-de-lis symbol of the monarchy. But…they refrained from melting down the metal pipes into bullets during the war after heeding pleas from Notre Dame's organ master, Claude Balbastre, who had adapted to new political realities by composing variations on the Marseillaise anthem."

Later, during the 19th century, Aristide Cavaille-Coll added to the great instrument, rebuilding parts damaged during the French Revolution and adding more pipes. Today, the organ is in no way behind the times, and it features a "new wooden-paneled console [with] five cascading keyboards and more than 200 stops." The *Associated Press* article continued, "A century ago, six strong men were needed to pump enough air for the music. Now, there is an air compressor behind the scenes, and the newly rebuilt instrument itself has a touch-screen panel that can note "favorite" stop combinations like a browser bookmarks a Web page. …refurbished for the cathedral's 850th anniversary this year [,] each of the nearly 8,000 pipes — some of which date back to the 18th century — was individually cleaned and returned to its place. The new electronic panel, the five cascading keyboards and more than 200 stops were installed."

Philippe Lefebvre is one of four *titulaires des grands orgues*, that is, head organists, at Notre

Dame. This assignment is considered something of a "holy grail," for organists, as it is one of the most prestigious posts of its kind in Europe. In speaking of his role, he once said, "Notre Dame's organ is particular because it is one of the only organs that has retained the traces of centuries. As the cathedral itself. So at the same time you have tones from before the Revolution, some from the 19th century similar to a symphonic orchestra, and also all the recent inputs of the 20th century. You have three or four authentic centuries of music. It resonates in the stones of the cathedral. ... Here in Notre Dame, when you play a tone, it resonates for eight to nine seconds. It is exceptional — the sound spreads across the whole structure, and you feel it when you play. The sound just comes back to you." As of this writing, the organ at Notre-Dame consists of nearly 8,000 pipes, more than 10% of them historical. It has 110 stops, five key boards and a 32-key pedalboard.

No one who has read Victor Hugo's famous novel, or even just seen the Disney version of *The Hunchback of Notre Dame*, can forget the scene of Quasimodo dancing and swinging among the cathedral's famous bells. There are 10 of them, and the oldest, and largest, is Emmanuel, which was cast for the church in 1681. It is the only one of the original bells to survive the French Revolution. Weighing 13 tons, it hangs from a solid beam in the south tower and tolls the hours of each day. It is also always the first to ring, leading the other nine bells like a choir master. On August 24, 1944, it rang alone, informing the people of Paris that Allied soldiers were on their way to liberate the city.

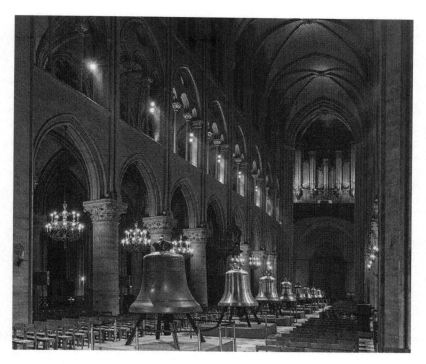

Myrabella's picture of Notre-Dame's bells on public display

For much of the 19th century and all of the 20th century, the next four bells hung in the north tower. They began on wheels, with ropes attached that allowed ringers to sound them. Later, they were attached to electric motors that allowed ringers to control them with the push of a button. However, as the building grew older, the size and strength of these four bells began to cause the entire cathedral to shake when they were played, making such a concert a rare event. In 2012, they were removed altogether and replaced with eight other bells cast in the same Normandy foundry that had produced the four 19th century bells in 1856. One more bell, larger than the other eight but not as large as Emmanuel, was added to the south tower, bringing the total to 10. Speaking for the cathedral, Regis Singer explained, "So, for the 850th anniversary of the cathedral, we wanted to reconstitute the ringing sound as it existed in the ancien regime, just before the revolution. We were able to do this by studying the bells in the church archives, all the way back to the 1300s. We could see their weight, thickness and diameter. And with these figures we were able to establish what they must have sounded like."

As had been mentioned before, Notre-Dame is, by design, full of statues. Among these, however, there is none perhaps as important as that of the Madonna and Child, which occupies a place of honor in the cathedral. Known as the Virgin of Paris, it was commissioned in the early 14th Century and remains an important symbol not just of the Virgin Mary's love for her Son, but also of, in the eyes of many, her love for the city of Paris. Writing at the turn of the 20th century, the famous author Hillaire Belloc observed, "It is a kind of core and centre to the city, and is, as it were, the genius catching up the spirit of the wars, and giving the generation of the last siege and reconstruction, as it will give on in the future to others in newer trials, a figure in which all the personality of the place is stored up and remembered. It was made just at the outbreak of the Hundred Years' War, it received the devotion of Etienne Marcel, it heard the outcry that followed the defeat of Poictiers and the captivity of the king…It has been for these five hundred years and more the middle thing, carrying with full meaning the name "Our Lady of Paris," which seems to spread out from it to the church and to overhang like an influence the whole city, so that one might wonder sometimes as one looked at it whether it was not the figure of Paris itself that one saw. It is the emblem of all that Paris has been, of its religion, of its civic ideals, of all that varied message which fails unceasingly and seems continually lost, as a ship—and a ship is also the symbol of Paris—seems to be lost in the trough of a high sea, and is hidden for a time but in the end is saved."

Carlos Delgado's picture of the statue of Mary in Notre-Dame

Online Resources

Other books about French history by Charles River Editors

Other books about Notre-Dame on Amazon

Further Reading

Bruzelius, Caroline. "The Construction of Notre-Dame in Paris." Art Bulletin (1987): 540–569 in JSTOR.

Davis, Michael T. "Splendor and Peril: The Cathedral of Paris, 1290–1350." The Art Bulletin (1998) 80#1 pp: 34–66.

Jacobs, Jay, ed. The Horizon Book of Great Cathedrals. New York City: American Heritage Publishing, 1968

Janson, H.W. History of Art. 3rd Edition. New York City: Harry N. Abrams, Inc., 1986

Myers, Bernard S. Art and Civilization. New York City: McGraw-Hill, 1957

Michelin Travel Publications. The Green Guide Paris. Hertfordshire, UK: Michelin Travel Publications, 2003

Temko, Allan. Notre-Dame of Paris (Viking Press, 1955)

Tonazzi, Pascal. Florilège de Notre-Dame de Paris (anthologie), Editions Arléa, Paris, 2007, ISBN 2-86959-795-9

Wright, Craig. Music and ceremony at Notre Dame of Paris, 500–1550 (Cambridge University Press, 2008)

Free Books by Charles River Editors

We have brand new titles available for free most days of the week. To see which of our titles are currently free, click on this link.

Discounted Books by Charles River Editors

We have titles at a discount price of just 99 cents everyday. To see which of our titles are currently 99 cents, click on this link.

Made in the USA
Middletown, DE
28 December 2019